# BELLEVUE
# MEMOIRS

## JOHN BEAULIEU, PH.D.

*Dedicated*

*to my patients —*

*they are my best teachers.*

# CONTENTS

# BIG APPLE
# PROLOGUE

Welcome to New York City!

The third day on the job, as part of my Bellevue orientation, I visited Manhattan State Hospital on Wards Island. I was told to take a taxi and to be sure to get a receipt for reimbursement. I was 25 years old and had never taken a taxi in my life. I was excited. I went down to First Avenue and 30th Street and put my hand into the air. Almost immediately, a yellow cab appeared. The cab swerved from the middle lane and nearly ran into another car, as well as running over me, before it stopped. I got in and told the driver I was going to Manhattan State Psychiatric Hospital.

The cab driver was wired. He activated the meter and we took off. I was thrown back into my seat as he accelerated. He weaved in and out of traffic as he constantly gave me details of what he was going to do. He would say, "I am going to take this guy on the right and get past him and then we will make this light." He would speed up, slow down, curse, scream, weave in and out of traffic, and simultaneously give me updates about what he was going to do.

Somehow we got to Manhattan State Psychiatric Hospital. I remember he pulled up too fast and slammed on his breaks. He was proud and held out his hand for his money and a tip. I was flush with adrenaline from the ride. I told him that I had raced motorcycles in Indiana, and that was nothing compared to his cab ride. He said, "Welcome to New York!" and took my money. I said, "I need a receipt." He ripped the receipt from the meter and threw it at me. He was in a hurry. It took three months until I risked another cab ride.

## A NEW YORK MINUTE

When I arrived at Bellevue Psychiatric Hospital from Indiana, I talked with a slow Indiana twang. The culture and pace of New York City was not familiar to me. It did not take long for me to realize that I needed to make adjustments. I talked so slowly that my patients would lose focus, hallucinate, and talk with the faster voices in their heads. It got to be funny. I would be explaining something important and patients would start talking with someone who was not there.

The problem was that I could not hear myself. Gertrude Schattner, our Drama Therapist, told me I needed to enunciate more clearly. Although Gertrude had lived in New York for many years, she spoke with a German accent. I had never heard a German accent, other than in the movies, so I could not understand a lot of what Gertrude was saying. It was frustrating and at the same time Gertrude was not about to give up on me.

One day Gertrude was watching me talk with a group of patients. Afterwards she said in her commanding German accent, "Sit, John!" I immediately sat down and she sat opposite me. She said, "I have the solution for you. Watch my hand going up and down. Every time it reaches the top, say a word, and when it reaches the bottom, say a word." It was brilliant. She would say, "Here is your Indiana tempo," and move her hand slowly. Next she would give me a New York tempo by moving her hand much faster. I practiced with her every day for weeks until I felt comfortable talking in a New York tempo.

What I did not expect was the effect that speeding up the tempo of my speech would have on my life as a New Yorker. Before my work with Gertrude, I was overwhelmed and I was thinking about going back to Indiana. I was having trouble adapting to the culture of New York City. I thought everyone was rude and that no one took their time to listen.

I discovered that speeding up my speaking also speeded up my life rhythm. I began to merge with New York City. I began liking the quick pace. Thoughts of leaving disappeared and at some point I became a New Yorker. I loved the city. I learned to talk faster and louder, be rude if necessary, honk my car horn more, and to not take it personally if people around me did the same thing. It was amazing.

## GOING HOME

A year later, I flew back to Indiana. When I got off the plane, I thought everyone was speaking in slow motion. It was like being on a drug. After an hour I remember a "pop" feeling and I slowed down to my Indiana tempo. Things were getting back to normal until I visited my friends. They all talked with accents. I had grown up with them but had never noticed their accents. Then I realized, "I talk like that. It's no wonder my patients in New York didn't understand me."

When I got back to New York I naturally speeded up. I am reminded of a Star Trek episode where Captain Kirk drinks alien water that speeds him up. He goes so fast that he disappears in normal time and reappears in "fast time." In fast time everything seems normal and he has to remember that he is moving at hyper speeds. After he successfully meets the alien challenge, he drinks the "slow-down water" and reappears in normal time. This is what was like for me in the beginning, going back and forth from New York City to Indiana.

Today, I live in the country in upstate New York. I usually go to sleep at 11 PM, the very latest. When I go into New York City to work, I go to sleep at 2 AM. As I get closer to the city I can feel myself speed up. I have learned over the years that a "New York Minute" is a very accurate description of New York City reality. When I get home I feel like Captain Kirk. I went into "fast time," did my work with the fast people, and came back to normal time.

## MY FIRST BAGEL

When I came to New York City I didn't know anything about Jewish culture. Mordecai, a therapist that I supervised, was an Hassidic Jew. I did not know he was Hassidic. I thought he was a hippie with his black clothes, tassels, and large black hat. When I saw more people dressed like Mordecai, I thought he was part of a commune. One day I asked Mordecai where his commune was at. He thought this was the funniest thing he had ever heard. After that Mordecai became my friend and my guide to the Jewish culture of New York.

During our talks, he mentioned that we should get some bagels. I said, "What's a bagel?" He looked at me like I was from another planet. He exclaimed, "You don't know what a bagel is?!" He told the Bellevue staff that I didn't know what a bagel was. At the next staff meeting there was a large tray piled with bagels. I looked at the bagels and thought, "What's the big deal—bread donuts." Then I took a bite of my first bagel and everyone celebrated. I love bagels and to this day whenever I eat a bagel I remember that celebration.

# INTRODUCTION

*BELLEVUE MEMOIRS* is about my experiences as an Activity Therapist with patients and staff in three different psychiatric hospitals from 1968-77. I began my career as an intern at Central State Psychiatric Hospital in Indianapolis, Indiana, from 1968-69. I did my residency as a staff therapist at Richmond State Psychiatric Hospital in Richmond, Indiana, from 1970-71, and I served as an Activity Therapy Supervisor at Bellevue Psychiatric Hospital in New York City from 1973-77.

Activity Therapists spend years perfecting their craft. My college studies included courses in counseling, leadership, group dynamics, psychology, anatomy, research, theory, and philosophy. When I completed my graduate work at Indiana University in 1973, I was hired by New York University with a special grant to design and research community transition programs at Bellevue Psychiatric Hospital. I spent hours creating, documenting, and researching different programs. I was directly responsible for training and supervising over forty therapists, nurses, and aides. I taught them how to successfully manage patient–community transition programs. Everything we did was researched, and every action we took was for the benefit of the patient.

An activity therapist works in real-life situations which requires specialized patient contact. They are sometimes with patients for hours in groups both inside and outside the hospital. The therapy room can be a hospital ward or outside the hospital in a movie theater, walking down the street, taking public transportation, or sitting in a park.

When I left Bellevue, I taught Activity Therapy and Counseling at City University of New York and Fairleigh Dickinson University. I started my own school in 1981 to teach innovative approaches to Body-Mind Therapy. Every time I tell a story about my hospital experiences to my students, I seek to honor my patients. Each story has a personal meaning for me because I lived through the experience. I know from my teaching experience that the stories hold a seed of truth for all of us. They teach us about honoring other peoples' realities, how to be flexible and compassionate, as well as how to meet life's challenges. So, with the encouragement of my students, I have written these stories. It is my hope that you will enjoy them, have meaning for you, and contribute to your life.

—John Beaulieu, Ph.D.

# INITIATION

MY FIRST VISIT to a psychiatric hospital was in April of 1969 as part of a class field trip to observe how activity was used as therapy. I was 21 years old, a new father, and very much a child of the 60's. I was looking forward to the field trip as an opportunity to get away, rather than for an educational experience. I remember getting a great sleep riding in the van on the way to Indianapolis, Indiana.

When our class arrived at Central State Psychiatric Hospital in Indianapolis, I was reminded of a high school experience. During my freshman year (1962), our school bus drove past Central State Hospital. There were always patients sitting on the benches behind a large chain-link fence. We would stick our heads out the bus window, make faces, and try to get a reaction from them. Mostly, they would just sit and stare into space as though we didn't exist. Every now and then someone would do something bizarre. One time a man in pajamas pulled down his pants and everyone on the bus went wild. We talked about this for weeks. He had inspired the kids on the bus to do even more bizarre acts as we passed by the hospital.

Central State Psychiatric Hospital
Administration Building

Central State Psychiatric Hospital opened in 1848 and was called Indiana Hospital for the Insane. The hospital consisted of one brick building situated on a large parcel of land and numbered over one hundred acres on the outskirts of Indianapolis. From 1848-1948, the hospital grew until it encompassed two massive ornate buildings. These buildings housed both female and male patients, and it also included a "sick" hospital for the treatment of physical ailments. There was a farm colony where patients engaged in occupational therapy, a chapel, an amusement hall complete with an auditorium with billiards and bowling alleys, a bakery, a fire house, a cannery manned by patients, and a pathology and autopsy lab. This was all surrounded by idyllic gardens and fountains.

Seven years later, I found myself in a van pulling into the grounds of the hospital. I was now on the other side of the chain-link fence. I thought we had entered a park because the grounds were spacious and well cared for. We passed by several ancient looking red brick buildings and pulled up to a new building. The sign on the building read "Hospital Administration." Two women welcomed us and we began our tour.

The first building we visited was an old surgical amphitheater built in the late 1800's. When we walked in the door, I thought I had gone back in time. In the center of the room was a steel surgical table, and on the walls behind the table were dark mahogany shelves filled with jars of preserved brains from mental patients. Facing the table and jars of brains were about fifty chairs ascending in five rows of ten chairs each. The floor was a cold tile designed to handle spilled blood and chemicals. Each jar was labeled for a suspected pathology of the brain. The building was preserved as a museum; however, few people knew about it. I was so impressed that I wrote the following poem when I returned home. I believe it best describes my feelings in that building.

## PATHOLOGY

I explored a part of my head,
Lost in the dust of bodies past.
Where lies preserved in a jar,
The dissected brains of the dead.

Each nicely labeled, classified, and categorized,
Displaying its glory from a mahogany shelf.
Silently swimming in chemical brine,
Which is fitted, sized, and personalized.

And somehow I can't help but hear,
Screams of agony and suffering of lives gone by,
Coming from behind some closed door,
Crossing and opening my closed ears.

Then looking into the darkened dinge,
The voices retreated into cracked walls.
But while I explored that one ancient shelf,
They whispered that someday they
would get their revenge.

Leaving the ghosts to decay,
Passing off their whispered chant,
Curiously following the brown light,
Into the place of the doctors' arcade.

Greeted by spirits of great stature,
Lecturing from behind their sacred altar,
To the wispy shadows of diseased colleagues,
About the brain of some cadaver on a slab.

Such a good deed the doctors did,
To look into the mind of their fellow man,
And remove it from his cracked head,
Before he was permanently committed to the dead.

And then I heard myself paged,
By someone alive and warm,
That the time had come to leave,
Where once the scalpel raged.

So I left wanting to stay,
And visit with those of the grave,
Leaving their shadows behind,
Calling it an interesting day.

By the time we left the surgical amphitheater, I was awake and excited.

We were then taken to a room to observe an Activity Therapy session. The activity for the morning was a patient square dance. The patients were supposed to move in a simple pattern with the music. Instead they were walking in random patterns, staring into space and/or talking to themselves. One man was talking about stoplights being a government conspiracy. Another woman was mumbling something about her cat.

An unshaven man in green hospital pajamas boldly walked up to me and said, "Do you have a match?" as his eyes rolled back in his head.

I said, "No."

He did an abrupt about face and stormed away as though I were the worst person in the world.

The therapist said, "Don't mind him. That's Earl. He's always like that."

There was something about these people that I liked. I felt a calling to work with them. When the time came to leave, my classmates couldn't wait to get out. I, on the other hand, couldn't wait to go back. On that day, I knew that I would complete my degrees and prepare myself to work with them.

Next, we visited the patient dormitories. These were the old red brick buildings we passed coming into the grounds. They were built between 1875 and 1900. I looked out a window and saw a graveyard across a road filled with old crosses. The graveyard was overgrown with weeds and not visible from the grounds. An older nurse noticed me looking at the graveyard and told me that in the old days when patients died, their bodies were taken past the dorms to the cemetery late at night.

She looked at me with the strangest eyes, as though she were in another world, and said, "They sure did howl when we brought those bodies by on a full moon." I immediately felt shivers up and down my spine and to this day the image still haunts me.

I was still determined. When I got back to school, something had changed inside me. I had a sense of focus. I sat with my advisor, Professor Johnson, and said, " I want to be a therapist and work in psychiatric hospitals." He said that I would have to take more psychology courses. I said, "No problem." Through all the disruptions of the sixties and being a new father, I managed to keep my focus, raise my grade average, and graduate.

# UNUSUAL
# TEACHERS

## BIG BEAR

I N ALL MY YEARS working as a therapist in psychiatric hospitals, I came to the realization that my patients were my teachers. To this day, their lessons continue to enrich and bring new dimensions to my life. From a psychiatric perspective, they were depressed and diagnosed with schizophrenia, bipolar depression, paranoid delusions, and personality disorders. Beyond these labels, I knew them as wonderful, creative, powerful, intuitive, insightful, and caring human beings. They were people who came to an edge, and crossed that fine line between sanity and insanity.*

---

*The exception to this were the sociopaths (now termed personality disorders) and psychopaths. They were in a group all by themselves. It took me many years to learn from them. However, to call them caring human beings would not be correct.

"Big Bear" was one of my favorite patients. I called him Big Bear because he was a big man with a heart like a teddy bear. I documented Big Bear's shifts between twenty-six different personalities over a period of many past lifetimes. He loved being called Big Bear because in one of his lives he was a shaman or spiritual teacher using bear magic. Big Bear was diagnosed as having multi-undifferentiated schizophrenia. Today we might call him a multiple personality; however, according to Big Bear these were his different lives.

Time meant nothing to Big Bear. This was one of the reasons he was hospitalized. He would walk the streets of Richmond, Indiana, at 4 AM talking with invisible people from different times. I later learned that this type of behavior was considered normal in New York City. In Indiana, though, it was considered psychotic.

In my attempt to understand Big Bear, I kept records of his different personalities, lives, and conversations. Big Bear learned to trust me because I respected him and genuinely wanted to know about his lives rather than cure him. I enjoyed talking with Big Bear and listening to his voice and body movements switch as he went in and out of different lifetimes. At one moment he would be a machine gunner in WWII, and a few minutes later he would be a baker for King George.

There was never a dull moment when Big Bear was around. If I felt a little down he, would always "make my day." I used to walk up to him and say, "Big Bear! Who are you today?" He would smile a big smile and a twinkle would come in his eyes. Then suddenly he would switch his voice and body posture and say, "Get down, John, get down!"

"Why, Big Bear?" I would say.

"Because they're shooting arrows."

"Who's shooting arrows, Big Bear?"

"The Roman army!"

I would crouch down with Big Bear. He would look so serious. Then in a minute we would stand up. I would hug him and say, "Thanks for saving my life." He would smile and walk away very proud of himself.

The only difference between ourselves and the "Big Bears" of the world is that we have the ability to understand and act in accordance with the rules of society. In my opinion, Big Bear also knew the rules of society, but his lack of a normal time sense and his personality changes threatened people. So we hospitalized Big Bear. In places like New York City, "the city that never sleeps," Big Bear could walk around and talk to himself at all hours of the day and night. He would either look normal or most likely not even be noticed.

I knew Big Bear in 1970-71. I wonder whether or not we would hospitalize him today. I sometimes expect to come across a New Age publication and rediscover Big Bear as a celebrity helping others recall their past lives. I remember talking with Big Bear when he was a Buddhist priest from the fifteenth century. I said, "Do you know that most people are not aware of their other lives?"

He smiled and squinted his eyes and said, "They should listen and learn. Bless them."

I said, "I can't remember my past lives."

Big Bear started to cry and placed his hand on my head. Then he said something which seemed like gibberish and I said, "Thank you."

Years later I read *Many Lives, Many Masters* by Dr. Brian Weiss. Dr. Weiss is a psychiatrist who did not believe in past lives. During a psychotherapy session, his patient began spontaneously recalling her past lives. Dr. Weiss decided to go along with it. In the end it was the patient who inspired Dr. Weiss to expand his view of therapy and reality. His patient became his teacher.

I do not know, nor do I believe anyone knows, the source of mental illness. I do believe that much of what we call mental illness stems from poverty and homelessness. Many of my patients became "crazy" as winter set in. They were great actors and could fool the best psychiatrists and therapists. Bellevue Psychiatric, located in the center of New York City, required an immense acting talent to get in. The competition was tough.

When I worked at Richmond State Hospital in Indiana, we admitted a woman who was delusional and constantly talked to herself. Her family said that she wandered through the streets late at night and they could not control her. One day I was sitting with her on the ward and she said, "I am so happy to be here. When I was in New York, I tried to get into Bellevue and they refused me."

I said, "Why!" in a shocked way.

She said, "I wasn't crazy enough so I just walked the streets for several years. I had a lot of street friends, but I always wanted to be in the hospital."

I remember asking myself the question, "I wonder what kind of patients they let in?" Little did I know that three years later I would be a therapist at Bellevue and a resident of New York City. After one year of living in New York City, my idea of sanity would undergo a radical shift.

The general view in a psychiatric hospital is that the patients are sick and the staff is well. I felt isolated when I began to relate to my patients in a different way other than "sick and well." There was no one to talk with about my insights and feelings. I remember talking with my supervisor and he said, "John, you are identifying too closely with your patients. This is not good. Just do your job. You don't need to know them."

After several encounters with my supervisors, I learned to keep my thoughts and experiences to myself. I did not accept the rigid sick/well distinction in their paradigm. I knew my job and I knew my patients needed my help and skill. I also knew that they were wonderful people and that having contact with them was important.

One day I went to Grand Rounds at New York University Hospital. This had a profound effect on my career. Grand Rounds took place in a large auditorium. During Grand Rounds, doctors and therapists present their research, case studies, and ideas. Grand Rounds was usually boring and a great place to get away and take a nap.

On this day, as I sat in the back of the auditorium preparing to doze off, I thought, "This is odd, everyone is looking to the stage, but no one is there." I sat up and saw two men under a table. One of them came out from under the table, took the microphone off the speakers' podium, and placed it under the table. I heard one say, "People were chasing you down the street." Then the other said, "Do you know them?"

The conversation went on for twenty minutes. I had woken up and totally forgot about taking a nap. During that time, the majority of the doctors and therapists got up and left. After forty minutes, there were just five of us left and we came to the stage and sat around the table. I still didn't know what was going on. I just knew I had to be there.

One man, who I guessed was the therapist, said to the other man, "It's time to go. Don't worry, I'll look out for those people you described. I know them now."

The man who was apparently the patient said, "Thank you. Just be careful."

A nurse came up to our little world around the table. The patient showed some hesitation. The therapist noticed her and said to the patient, "It's OK, she's on your side." The patient smiled and walked away with her on his way back to the ward.

The mysterious therapist introduced himself as Dr. R.D. Laing, a visiting psychiatrist from England. The patient was from one of our wards, and Dr. Laing was demonstrating his method of getting into a patient's reality. He told us that we must honor a patient's reality before we can know anything about him. He told us stories about sitting in closets for hours talking with schizophrenic patients in order to understand their view of the world.

The more he talked, the more I wanted to cry. All those years of hiding my feelings for my patients and thinking something was wrong with me for respecting and honoring their reality began to release. I realized that someone understood and was publicly speaking out for a shift in our attitudes towards patients. When I realized how few people stayed to hear his words, I knew the courage it took Dr. Laing to come forth and present his views.

I have always shared my experiences in psychiatric hospitals with my students. Every time I tell a story, I seek to honor my patients and extract a "learning nectar" from the experiences we had together. Every story has a personal meaning for me. The same stories also hold a seed of truth for all of us. They illustrate important points about honoring another's reality, flexibility, compassion, creativity, and a readiness to accept challenge. They also engage us in all of our feelings.

I am fully aware that my patients needed professional assistance and I trained many years to help them. I also know that regardless of their depression and confusion, they are also caring, loving human beings. Through all the schizophrenia, psychopathic behavior, autism, bipolar depression, and compulsions that my patients exhibited, I found them to be some of the best teachers and friends I have ever found.

# PAYING MY DUES

## RICHMOND STATE
## PSYCHIATRIC HOSPITAL

AFTER GRADUATING from Purdue University, I did a residency at Richmond State Psychiatric Hospital in Richmond, Indiana. Richmond State is a large state hospital located on 307 acres. Their doors opened in 1890 under the name of Eastern Indiana Hospital for the Insane. When I arrived in 1970, the hospital was in the process of discharging as many long term institutionalized patients as possible. The hospital was designed to be isolated from the community. At one time patients farmed and prepared their own food, and the hospital was nearly self-sustaining. Many of the older patients called the hospital home and did not want to go back into the community.

Richmond State was the perfect place to gain a lot of experience. The hospital was understaffed and the job responsibilities tended to overlap. I often found myself in situations that were not remotely related to my university training. I quickly learned to adapt and be creative. I took every opportunity to learn new skills in order to become more knowledgeable. I befriended the chief psychologist, Dr. John Parrish, who became my supervisor, mentor, and guide. Dr. Parrish established an in-service training program in which I learned practical behavioral psychology skills, basic cognitive therapy, and a complete program of gestalt therapy. It was here that I experienced my first encounter group. Dr. Parrish loved music and together we formed a folk band, performed for the patients, and established a rudimentary music therapy program.

## FULL MOON

I remember leaving the hospital late one July night and looking up at a full moon. The evening was very quiet and I felt surrounded by the ghosts of patient's past. As I walked through the buildings, still filled with patients, I heard a scream. Then all was quiet again.

## SCHIZOPHRENIC BOWLING

Richmond State Psychiatric Hospital had a patient's recreation room with a one-lane bowling alley. I was bowling with a group of acute schizophrenic patients. That in itself was quite a feat. For example, one patient decided that it would be better to roll the ball into the card tables of the recreation room. I stopped him just as he was about to release the ball.

However, the story of this one particular day was about Edward. Edward was a 40-year-old mentally challenged man who had spent most of his life in the hospital. Edward liked to please people and everyone liked Edward. Our bowling alley needed pin setters and Edward was our man for this day. To start, each bowling pin needed to be placed on a special mark to make a symmetrical triangle. This of course was too much for Edward. What made this even more interesting was that the patients rarely noticed Edward's odd pin setting patterns. On this day, however, Edward was in rare form.

Edward was setting pins when a patient sitting at the card tables had a heart attack. I rushed over and began CPR. The other patients were in shock and started walking around in circles talking to themselves. A nurses' aide ran for help. After several minutes of CPR, a doctor arrived and took over. The patient was going to be all right.

However, when I went back to the bowling alley, my patients were clearly agitated. At the same time they were still bowling. I couldn't believe it. When I sat down, my adrenaline was still pumping from the CPR. I just wanted to close my eyes for a moment. Then I saw it.

Edward had risen to a new level of pin setting. During the mayhem he had become excited and misplaced a bowling pin. So instead of looking for it, Edward had decided to use his head as a bowling pin. When I saw what was happening, the bowling ball was already on its way. I yelled just as the ball hit Edward on the top of his head. I heard it go "gonk."

I ran to Edward, my mind working a mile a minute. Meanwhile, the patients were preparing to roll another ball. When I got to Edward I lifted him up. He looked woozy and then he said, "Did I do good?" At that moment another ball ripped through the remaining pins. Edward laughed. The patients laughed. I laughed.

## SINK OR SWIM

One day, the head of the department came to me and said, "John, the city has given us the use of a local pool to take our patients swimming from 9 to 10:30 AM three times a week. Since you are our only staff therapist with a Red Cross Lifeguard and Water Safety Instructor Certificate, you have been nominated to take them."

The following week I went to the pool with two aides and one other therapist. Neither aide could swim. The other therapist was against the whole idea and felt forced to go. We took five disturbed children and six disturbed adults. I soon realized that nothing in my Red Cross training even remotely prepared me for this lifeguard/therapist assignment.

My plan was to put the children in the junior pool and to contain the adults in the three foot section of the large pool. Within minutes the children were out and the adults were heading for the diving boards. I blew my whistle in an attempt to get control. It didn't work. My adrenaline was clearly beginning to surge.

Fortunately, most of the adult patients had some sense of safety—they began playing in the five foot water and stopped before they got to the diving board. The children, however, wanted to go off the diving board. I was yelling at the aides and the other therapist to head them off. The patients were running and some were beginning to throw major tantrums.

Two children got through our defenses. One climbed up the three meter board, walked out to the end, and began laughing and talking to himself. Simultaneously, an autistic girl jumped into the ten foot water and literally sank to the bottom. I went in after her. When I got to the bottom of the diving pool, she was talking underwater. Bubbles were coming out of her mouth. I couldn't believe it.

I immediately grabbed her and brought her to the surface. As we broke the water line, she inhaled and continued to talk nonsense. She had no idea what had happened and wanted to go back.

I then looked up at Kevin on the diving board. He was still laughing and talking to himself. No one would climb the board to get him down. It was up to me. When I got to the end of the board, I realized that there was only one safe way out. That was straight down. I would much rather him fall into the water than on concrete.

I crawled out on the board like a cat stalking its prey. Then without hesitation, I grabbed Kevin, and we fell ten feet into the water. He never stopped talking and laughing all the way down. I dragged him to the side of the pool, and he was as happy as could be. "What fun!"

Although we had another hour at the pool, I decided to herd them into the van and just drive around. When we returned to the hospital, my boss asked me why I looked so tired. For the next four weeks, the assistant staff members and I agreed to just drive around in the van for an hour and then return to the hospital. We wrote the city a thank you letter for the use of their pool which was published in the local newspaper—it was an election year.

## DR. W'S CREDIT CARD

Johnny was diagnosed as a CSP which means criminal sexual psychopath. He was just 25 years old and committed to a locked ward for one year for observation. He enjoyed exposing himself to everyone. Apparently, one day in a small Indiana town he exposed himself to the town judge and his family as they were leaving church.

Johnny was the first psychopath I had ever worked with. At our team meetings Dr. W, who you will hear more about later, wasn't very interested in what anyone had to say. I reported that I questioned Johnny's hospitalization at a team meeting. Dr. W looked at me and said, "Of course, he is a psychopath." That was the end of it.

Well, Johnny kept working on me. I got permission to take him on walks around the grounds. Dr. W just signed the paper without even looking. After three weeks of listening to him make a case for himself, I was convinced he was sane. One day, I looked the other way and he escaped.

Dr. W seemed unconcerned. He said these things happen and the police would find him. Then one day at team meeting, Dr. W seemed more concerned. He looked at me with his deep penetrating psychiatrist's eyes and dropped a paper on the table in front of me.

It was a bill from his credit card company. Apparently, Johnny, before leaving, had stopped by Dr. W's office and stole all his credit cards. Dr. W didn't notice. Now, one month later, we all sat looking at a bill of ten thousand dollars. Most of the charges were in California. Johnny had somehow managed to get from Indiana to California.

To his credit, Dr. W looked at me and said, "Now, you have learned what a psychopath is. How does it feel?" He didn't want a reply. He stood up and left the room.

Johnny was returned two weeks later. I asked him why he had stolen the credit cards from Dr. W. He said that Dr. W could afford it and had suggested to him that it was OK. Since he was in the wrong place, he knew that Dr. W would want him to have a good time. As he spoke, part of me wanted to believe him. It even seemed plausible. However, the contrast between the facts and his ability to manipulate were crystal clear. Johnny was my first psychopath friend and teacher. I have never forgotten him.

## SUPER BEE GETS RELIGION

"Super Bee" was a 9-year-old schizophrenic boy. He talked of monsters in his dreams and threw wild tantrums. One day, a local church group of "nice ladies" invited the children to a special party at their church. They were showing drawings and paintings made by hospital patients. Super Bee and several of the other children were among the artists whose paintings were on display.

Super Bee could care less about his painting. He was walking around trying to grab as much candy as he could. It was at this time a woman from the church walked up to Super Bee and said, "Aren't you a nice little boy!"

I knew Super Bee well, and this lady had no idea what she was getting into. Super Bee looked up at her with his sweet little boy face and she gave him a big smile. Super Bee then said in a loud continuous voice, "You stupid bitch, fuck you, up your ass, eat shit, mother fucker cock sucker turd eater, fuck, fuck, fuck, shit." He continued with his cursing trance for a good two minutes as she stood paralyzed. Super Bee had no idea what was going on around him, nor did he have any idea he was shocking the church lady. The whole scene had the quality of some strange childhood innocence.

Suddenly, Super Bee stopped cursing as he saw some interesting candy. The church lady's mouth was moving but nothing was coming out. I walked over to her and said, "Isn't he such a nice boy?" as though I had not seen what had just happened.

Her eyes blurred and she somehow managed to reply in her sweet voice and say, "Yes." Needless to say, she kept away from Super Bee for the rest of the party.

## SCHIZOPHRENIC BASKETBALL

In Indiana, everyone plays basketball, including the schizophrenics and epileptics. I was assigned to be the coach of the Richmond State Psychiatric Hospital's basketball team. We held practice every day, and everyone wanted the patients to win. What they were winning was a game in a basketball league consisting of teams from different state mental hospitals. I know that sounds crazy, and as you'll find out, you're right!

Our practices were, at best, a little odd. In those days, the patients were often heavily medicated. They would stop in the middle of shooting or passing a ball, stare into space, or just fall asleep. On the other end of the spectrum, they might have auditory or visual hallucinations. During practice, one patient kept throwing the ball into the bleachers. (Our hospital had a full basketball court with bleachers and people actually came from the community to see the games.

Administration Building at East Haven, Richmond, Ind.

State Asylum, East Haven—Richmond, Ind.

But that's another story.) I said, "Bob, just throw the ball to someone. It won't work to throw it in the air like that."

Bob looked at me with glazed eyes and said, "But the voice tells me that it's good luck to throw the ball into the air, and if I don't, someone can get hurt."

I thought, "OK, this ought to be good, especially with the other patients finding nothing unusual in Bob's behavior."

Our first game was scheduled with the state epileptic hospital. My team was in questionable shape. Besides me, there were two nurses, two nurses' aides, and a therapist, in addition to about twenty people from the community who had come to watch. I was asked to referee and was handed a whistle and several tongue depressors.

The game began with a whistle and, right at that moment, one of my patients started to wander off. At that same time, another one had a grand mal seizure. In those days, the recommended procedure was to stabilize the patient's head and to insert a tongue depressor in his mouth. A nurse immediately ran out and did this. In the meantime, my patients were walking around talking to themselves. It took fifteen minutes to get everyone back together.

I blew the whistle and the game began again. It was exciting and everyone clapped. Five minutes into the game another patient had a grand mal seizure and a nurse ran out and stabilized him. Next, as my patients began to roam, yet another patient had a seizure and then another. I stabilized the patient next to me. The rest of my patients, however, were "gone." I yelled at the nurses' aides to control them but between the seizures and patients wandering around hallucinating, we simply did not have enough staff to handle them.

Fortunately, many of my patients just went to the bleacher seats and the epileptic patients knew what was happening and were somewhat controlled. The aides managed to catch the few patients who had headed for the door. When I finally managed to get a good view of everything, it was funny to see my patients in the bleachers sitting with the "normal people." It was even funnier to see the expressions of the normal people who had just watched at least four grand mal seizures and patients walking around at random talking to themselves. It was at that moment that I realized that there is nothing that comes close to Indiana basketball and its fans.

## BAD CHILDREN

All the therapists were sitting in a team meeting listening to a male nurses' aide talk about the boys on the children's ward and their cursing. The aide was going on and on about how it had to be stopped. He kept quoting Jesus and the Bible. It was becoming questionable to all of us who was really disturbed here. When the man finished, he looked at Dr. W and said, "We just have to do something about this."

Dr. W looked right back at him and said, "No Fuck!"

The aide left without saying another word.

Dr. W looked at me and smiled.

## THE BLOW JOB

Every Friday night all the patients would come to the gymnasium for a big-screen movie. There would usually be about 40 to 50 patients. Usually, I would be on the main floor watching the patients along with several aides. On this night, however, the aide who usually ran the projector called in sick and I was on the balcony running it.

The movie was *Butch Cassidy and the Sundance Kid*. The gym was dark and we were near the middle of the movie. A sex scene was showing on the screen when I heard a loud scream coming from the middle of the group. The scream sent chills up my spine. I ran from the balcony and was on the floor in seconds. The aides were trying to figure out where the scream came from and the patients were beginning to panic. Finally, an aide turned on the lights and then I saw it. Marty, a severely mentally challenged man, was covered with blood and writhing on the floor.

I began to examine him and then the realization hit me. Bob, one of the other mental patients, had bit into Marty's penis during the sex scene. I opened his pants immediately and applied direct pressure. The whole scene was a bloody mess. Fortunately, the aides reacted fast and the patients were cleared out safely. We got a stretcher and took Marty over to the infirmary while I walked along holding direct pressure to his crotch.

As fate would have it, Dr. H was on call that evening. Dr. H was an alcoholic and when he arrived he was quite drunk. When he saw Marty and his penis he commented, "That was one hell of a blow job." Then he started to clean him up and, to his credit, he did a good job. I think Dr. H must have been running on pure instinct because the smell of alcohol from his breath was enough to get me drunk.

Dr. H called in Dr. W and they decided to suture Marty's penis back together. Dr. W said that he had done things like that during the war. They both had a drink from Dr. W's brandy flask and proceeded with their sewing project.

I visited Marty in the hospital every day. Marty wasn't even sure what had happened. When the bandages were removed, I couldn't help but notice that his penis was sewed together crooked. Dr. H said, "Marty, my man, you'll have to take it easy with that sword." Marty didn't know why, but he laughed. For weeks, everyone asked Marty to show them his penis. His friend Bob never figured out what he did and Marty really enjoyed the attention.

## CAMPING OUT
## (IT'S ALL A MATTER OF PERSPECTIVE)

I worked with mentally challenged and disturbed children. One day I decided to start a Boy Scout troop for them. I called the Boy Scouts of America and received permission.

They were very interested in the idea. As far as I know, it was the first scout troop for disturbed boys.

Our scout meetings were different from my scout days. My scout master Mr. K was an alcoholic and veteran of WWII. Our scout meetings with Mr. K were run like a Green Beret training camp. He was determined to make guerrilla fighters out of all of us. I remember an outing when the temperature dropped below zero. The night was freezing and Mr. K had rented the movie *Invasion of the Body Snatchers*. The movie was very frightening, and at the same time, I could not imagine leaving the warmth of the movie room.

I was determined to make my troop meetings different. I wanted to teach the boys basic survival skills. But since these skills could be dangerous for them—one boy had already burned down his parents' house and another most likely would use his knot tying skills for nefarious purposes—I decided instead to concentrate on hiking around the hospital, getting everyone into uniforms, and doing good deeds. One day, with the boys all dressed in their uniforms, we walked down the main street of town and picked up litter. The town reporter took a photo and wrote it up in the local paper. We were all very proud.

The local Boy Scout troop saw the article in the paper and decided to invite us to an outing at the Bear Creek campgrounds. This meant taking the boys out overnight and having them sleep in tents with hundreds of normal boys. We decided to go for it. That evening, after the campfire program of stories and skits, the boys were really happy. They were acting perfectly normal. Other boys began telling them about their lives and at the same time asked questions about the hospital. I don't know exactly what they all talked about, but they talked for hours.

When we had our next meeting at the hospital, I asked them to share their experiences of the camping trip. One boy looked at me with big blue eyes and said, "Mr. Beaulieu, I can't understand why those other boys aren't in the hospital." Then another boy said, "Mr. Beaulieu, I feel really safe in here. There are all these crazy boys out there."

## TOO MUCH WORK

When I was working at my first job as a therapist, I had no idea how to keep good time boundaries. During that summer with the Boy Scout troop and my other responsibilities, I was working 80+ hours a week and sometimes worked right through the weekend. I really wanted to make a difference and I loved my work. One day I felt funny. I walked into my supervisor Norm's office to talk about my scout program. Norm looked up and all I remember is saying, "Norm," and I collapsed on the floor. All I could think of was, "Please don't call Dr. H." I must have somehow asked Norm to drive me home because I woke up in my own bed. I went to our family doctor and he said I had collapsed from exhaustion and lack of sleep. He suspected

I had mononucleosis and recommended bed rest. Today we would call it burnout. I learned my lesson the hard way about how important it is to keep good time boundaries.

## ALCOHOLIC REMISSION

Dr. H was the head psychiatrist of the alcoholic ward and I was a young therapist on his team. I really did not understand much about alcoholism and certainly therapeutic knowledge of alcoholism has come a long way since 1970. However, I was gung-ho and ready to make a change. Every morning I would work with the alcoholics to motivate them to stop drinking by having them make sounds and do exercises. There is nothing like a group of drying out alcoholics doing exercise. Looking back, I have to say it bordered on the absurd.

Every morning after exercise we had a meeting with the staff and patients. All the patients loved Dr. H. He didn't say much, and I suspect they liked him because he allowed them a lot of freedom. On this particular morning, Dr. H was nowhere to be found. All the patients were sitting around a large table complaining as usual.

Since Dr. H was not there, I decided to give a speech on exercise and clean living. This was not well received, and most of them just moaned about the idea of more exercise and health food. Right in the middle of my speech Dr. H called in. We had just gotten a speaker phone. The nurse, without Dr. H's knowledge, put him on the speaker phone.

Dr. H said, "I got drunker than a skunk last night. I got a hangover you wouldn't believe and threw up all over my living room. Shit, I'm sick." His words were slurred and he continued, "I need a drink! What time is it anyway Tell the patients I won't be at the meeting today. I have a headache!" Then he hung up the phone. The alcoholics were ecstatic. They were hitting each other on the back and saying, "That Dr. H is one hell of a guy!" No one ever told Dr. H that he was on the speaker phone. I don't think he even remembered calling in.

## INCOGNITO

One day I asked Dr. H what he would do if he were driving down the highway and saw an accident. He said, "John, I always travel incognito."

## THORAZINE

I kept asking Dr. W during our team meetings to tell me what the drug Thorazine, a drug used to control psychiatric symptoms, was like, and why all the patients were taking so much of it. I was a young therapist, and Dr. W was in his late sixties. He had seen almost everything. Finally he said, "John, the only answer to your question is to take some." Having had some experience with drugs in the sixties, I was ready to try. I thought "Wow, Dr. W wants me to legally find out about a psychiatric drug."

Many patients were now taking 250mg of Thorazine four times a day. Dr. W gave me 100mg. I was disappointed. Two hours later I went to sleep in the middle of the day and woke up on the ward a day later. I thought it was the same day. Dr. W had called my wife and told her I was learning through an experience, so everything was all right.

When I woke up, Dr. W had a good laugh along with the rest of our team. They made jokes and talked about my inability to handle Thorazine for days. There is nothing like direct experience, and I have never asked or thought about taking a psychiatric drug again. However, the experience did give me a tremendous amount of empathy for my patients. I kept thinking how 100mg affected me and how they were taking so much more. I still think about this today.

## SCHIZOPHRENIC EXERCISE

William was diagnosed with catatonic schizophrenia. He was 14 years old and stared into space without speaking. When William was 9, his mother doused herself in gasoline and called William into her room. William walked through the door just in time to see his mother explode into flames.

I really liked William. Sometimes I would sit with him, and other times I would hold him. William learned my name, and every now and then he would lift his head and say, "Awwwww John" in a long drawn out tone. In a strange sort of way, William was my friend.

Three times a week William would come to exercise. There is nothing like exercising with a group of chronic schizophrenics. Calling it exercise is taking a great amount of liberty. I thought that throwing a ball back and forth would at least keep them alert. So I purchased a large light-weight ball, something like a beach ball but firmer. Everyone got in a circle, and we began to toss it around.

I would get a patient's attention and toss him the ball. For example, I would say, "Bob! Look at me! Here comes the ball!"

Bob looked my way, and I would think, "Great, I have his attention," and toss the ball to him. Before the ball would reach Bob, his attention would shift from the ceiling to the floor, or he would start talking to himself. The ball would bounce off Bob's head or body, and he would just continue talking to himself, or walk away as though nothing had happened.

My favorite exercise was jumping jacks. I would say, "OK, it's time for some jumping jacks! Let's line up."

Making any sort of a line was not possible. They would be walking all over the gym in random patterns. I would grab a patient and take him to the line and say, "OK, you stay right here and keep your feet on that line." Then I would go after another patient. My goal was to get all the patients standing on the line at once. After twenty sessions, I reached my goal for five seconds.

Getting them to the line was difficult enough. However, performing a jumping jack was another story. When I got tired of running around trying to get them to the line, I would grab one patient and say, "OK, let me see a jumping jack."

I remember Jack standing with his feet together and lifting his hands about six inches from his side. Bob would stand on his toes and come down. Ted would just rock back and forth. To my knowledge no one ever "jumped" or even approached anything like it.

Back to William. In the middle of all this chaos I would often decide to work with William. I would stand William on the line and lift his arms up and down. Then I would stand about five feet from him and bounce him the ball. The ball would bounce off William's belly and he would say, "Awwwww John."

This routine continued three times a week for nine months. One day I bounced the ball off William's belly, and he said in his long drawn out voice, "Stop that Johnnnnnnnn."

I couldn't believe what I had heard. I was so excited. William said something different. I ran over and hugged him. I must have squeezed him too tight. He said, "Stop that Johnnnnnnnn." I thought, "Wow, William is talking. This is great."

I left the hospital three months later. William continued to say "Stop that Johnnnnn" and "Awwwww

Johnnnnnnnn". I told William how much I would miss him. In a strange way, I had grown to love William, and William in his own catatonic schizophrenic way had come to love me. I tried to be strong and then I began to cry. William looked at me and said, "Awwwww John."

## LSD—PREPARING FOR BELLEVUE

I was working at the crisis intervention center at Indiana University three evenings a week as part of my graduate internship. My job primarily involved counseling runaways and working with depressed students and community members threatening suicide. One night, a man called high on LSD. I asked him to come in but he refused, saying, "They'll get me if I leave the room."

I asked who "they" were and he said, "They, you know, they."

I then asked him where he was, and to my surprise he was in a fraternity house five minutes away from our crisis center. I decided to check it out. I found him in a dark room with several frat brothers. They were all tripping on LSD.

I said, "Hi, I/m the guy you called on the phone at the crisis center. Is everyone all right? Do you need to talk?"

One of the frat brothers said, "Is it safe outside now?"

I asked him what he meant. He said, "You know, the little men who torture you. They were everywhere. Have they left?"

I said that I just walked over and hadn't seen any little men. They seemed relieved. Two started laughing and just left the room having a great time. However, one huddled even further into the corner.

I sat down near him and said, "Do you need help?"

He said he was afraid and lost. I suggested that we go for a walk. He agreed, and we went to a pond near the frat house. He seemed to calm down, and we sat there talking about life for over a half hour. Then all of a sudden he jumped up. Apparently, a police siren in the distance had scared him.

He began to shake and become agitated. He began saying, "They're coming! They're coming!" Before I could say anything, he started screaming and running down the middle of the street. His arms were flailing and waving wildly. I thought he might get hit by a car. My adrenaline surged, and I took off after him.

We ran for over two miles. He never stopped screaming and waving his arms. It was a miracle that he wasn't hit by a car because he ran down the middle of a major street against traffic. Horns were honking, and people were yelling which I am sure only added to his situation.

I finally caught up with him and made a desperate leap for his legs. Down he went. I jumped on top of him. He was wild, and his strength was more than I could have ever imagined. He literally flipped me into the air as though I were nothing. When I got up, he was running again.

I took off after him. He ran right across a major intersection, and then to my surprise, he ran right into the front door of our university hospital. He had no idea where he was and, as I entered the door, he began to yell and throw chairs around. The security guard grabbed him and I grabbed him and somehow we both managed to hold him.

A young intern appeared and before I knew it he had injected the young man with something I later learned was Valium. The intern then disappeared. In less than a minute the frat man was quiet and just staring at the wall.

I went looking for the doctor. When I found him he just said, "Another bad trip. I've seen fifteen tonight. I heard this one gave you a good chase." I heard a woman screaming and the intern looked at me, smiling, and said, "Busy night," and disappeared through a door.

Meanwhile, the frat brother was still looking at the wall. I said good-bye, and he just gave me a blank stare. The security guard at the door said, "Don't worry, he's out for the rest of the night." It was three in the morning, and I went home. I stared at the wall for over an hour and finally fell asleep. That wall looked pretty good at the time.

# BELLEVUE
# PSYCHIATRIC
# HOSPITAL

### THE BIG APPLE PRELUDE

WHEN I WORKED at Richmond Psychiatric Hospital, a woman told me a story I will never forget. I had never been to New York City at that time, but I had heard of Bellevue Psychiatric Hospital. We were sitting at a card table talking about what she would do when she left the hospital. She said how happy she was just to get into the hospital. There was no doubt in my mind or the minds of our team that this woman needed to be in the hospital. I asked her what she meant. She said that a year ago she was living in New York City. She started to see bugs on her walls and was unable to concentrate. She went to Bellevue Psychiatric and was refused admittance. They told her there were others in New York far more deserving of admittance than her. I remember thinking, "What kind of place is this."

## THE INTERVIEW

I arrived from Indiana in a Volkswagen bus. I had hair to my shoulders. I was dressed like a cowboy with my leather vest, plaid green shirt and string tie, and my best jeans for my interview at Bellevue Psychiatric. The first people I met were Jane and Sue. Jane was the Director of Activity Therapy and Sue was the Assistant Director of Activity Therapy. They knew I had come highly recommended with graduate degrees from Indiana and Purdue University. When they saw me, they smiled at each other.

We just sat there for what seemed like an eternity and said nothing. Suddenly, Sue left the room and Jane got up. There was a staff meeting down the hall, and Jane said it was time for me to meet the rest of the staff. When I walked into the room, everyone was laughing. Jane introduced me. Everyone just sat for several minutes and "felt my energy." I left in silence. Jane called me back the next day and told me I was hired.

## SUPERMAN MAN OF STEEL

Overwhelmed is the only word I can think of that summarizes my first experience in New York City. Having grown up in Indiana, I was not even remotely prepared for my new adventure. Somehow I managed to get up bright and early on Monday morning and go to my first day of work at Bellevue Psychiatric Hospital. I was told that members of the staff should enter the hospital through the back admitting entrance. As I rounded the corner, a man dressed like Superman jumped off a garbage can right in front of me. He spread his legs, dug his heels into the ground, and crossed his arms as though he were the most powerful man in the world.

I said, "Who are you?"

He looked shocked and with a very stern face and low voice he said, "I am the Man of Steel, and you may not enter."

I couldn't believe it. After the subway, walking through car horns honking, sirens blaring, and just trying to get to work, I am stopped by Superman. "Why isn't he in the hospital as a patient. What's going on?" I thought to myself.

I went into a door on my left and found the acute admitting office. I told the admitting psychiatrist who I was and that this was my first day on the job. I asked him about Superman and asked why he wasn't in the hospital. He

smiled, opened his desk drawer, and handed me three green rocks and said, "This should do it."

I walked back to the entrance and sure enough Superman jumped off his garbage can and stood in front of me. I opened my hand, and he saw the three green stones. He instantly fell backwards and held up his hands. I walked past him and entered the building reminding myself to carry my green "kryptonite" stones to work.

## A GOOD PORNO MOVIE
## "WE SEE WHAT WE WANT TO SEE."

Leisure transition groups were designed to help patients plan for and successfully use their free time. The basic idea behind these groups was to develop patient cooperation and responsibility. The leisure groups were structured in tiers. In the first tier, the patients met in the hospital and attended community activities. The second tier consisted of discharged patients who met in the community and attended activities together. Patients near discharge would be encouraged to attend second tier groups.

Second tier groups always researched and voted on the activity they wanted to attend. This particular evening the group voted to see a movie called *Emmanuelle* in the East Village. A basic assumption of the group was that members were adults and that therapists empowered them to choose activities. So we all prepared to go to see the movie *Emmanuelle*.

When we got to the movie, I discovered that *Emmanuelle* was an X-rated soft porn movie. My mind went crazy with thoughts. I kept thinking, "What if anyone sees me? Just let me get through this. What if a patient freaks out? What will happen to my professional reputation? Will the hospital put an end to my groups; they are working so well?" The thoughts went on and on.

We all got into the movie, and the patients wanted to eat popcorn and drink soda while watching the movie. I really don't remember much about the movie. Thank goodness it was soft porn. Since it was a new concept, the theater was nearly full. As strange as it sounds, I kept thinking we might be lost in the crowd.

In those days, movies had a short intermission. When the lights came on, a man sitting in front of us stood up and turned around. My heart skipped a beat, and I lost my voice. The man was Dr. B, the head psychiatrist from the ward the patients had been discharged from. Dr. B was wearing a Mickey Mouse tee shirt. He gave his "I've seen everything" shrink look. He looked at me and said, "Not a bad movie." I really do not know what I said. Then he looked at the patients and they were clearly happy to see him. They kept saying, "Hi, Dr. B," and so on. Then we all sat down and watched the rest of the movie. I mostly listened to my thoughts of having to answer to Dr. B the next day.

After the group experience, we always went to a cafeteria and talked before going back to the hospital. I couldn't imagine what they were going to talk about. I began our conversation with "Does anyone have anything to say about the movie?" as if it were a love story. To my surprise, no one talked about the sex. They all talked about the jeeps and the good weather. One man said his dream was to live in the Caribbean. After fifteen minutes, I couldn't take it and asked, "Did anyone notice the sex in the movie?" After all, the movie was 95 percent about sex. No one seemed to notice and thought my question was strange. So we left the cafeteria, and everyone went home happy except for me. I had to go to work the next day and face Dr. B and the staff.

After a restless night, I went into work. I went into our team meeting with my head hung in shame. When I sat at the table, Dr. B said that he saw a great movie, *Emmanuelle*. Everyone on the team agreed with him. They apparently had all seen it. Then Dr. B looked at me and said, "I bet the patients loved the weather and the jeeps."

## WILL THE REAL JESUS STAND UP PLEASE

When I was first developing the community transition program for Bellevue Psychiatric, I asked local churches for places to have meetings outside the hospital. All the churches were very cooperative. One church gave us an office with a very comfortable couch and chairs for meetings. It was, in fact, a very comfortable room except for one thing.

I was sitting in a large overstuffed chair talking with a group of four patients from the hospital. Two were sitting on a couch opposite me and the other two were in chairs facing me. As we began talking about how to organize evening plans, they seemed disinterested. After about ten minutes, I realized that they weren't even talking to me.

I couldn't figure out what was going on. One patient in particular just kept holding his hands up in prayer position and mumbling incoherent words. The others just kept looking above my head. It was the strangest feeling.

After twenty minutes passed, one patient began talking about the devil and another patient began to show signs of being agitated. A third got up with a lot of confidence and started saying, "Bless you, bless you, and be gone, Satan."

It was turning out to be a real circus. It got to the point that I thought it best to return to the hospital. I got up and as I turned to get my coat, I saw above my chair a large picture of Jesus. In a way I saw the light, because it was at that moment I understood what was going on.

I bowed to the picture of Jesus and turned to my patient on the couch who clearly believed he was Jesus Christ and said to him: "Father, thank you for the use of this room. It is truly a blessing."

He touched my head and said it was time to return to Jerusalem.

We all went back to the hospital in peace.

The next time we used the room I covered the picture of Jesus in advance and had them all face in a different direction. All went well.

## TACKLING A LIFE

I shared my first office at Bellevue Psychiatric with two other supervisors. The office overlooked 28th Street and the NY Medical Center morgue. My desk was opposite two very large windows. The window had no guards or screens. We were seven stories up.

It was a hot summer day, and I was alone in the office working at my desk. The windows and the door to the hallway were open. Across the hallway, patients were taken to receive X-rays for TB. On this day, a very obese woman shuffled into my office in pajamas. I didn't notice her until she began climbing up to the window.

I shot like a rocket over my desk and literally grabbed her love handles. She was just starting to fall forward. I leaned backwards, spread my legs for stability, propped my feet just below the window ledge, and pulled back with all my strength.

After what seemed like an eternity, I felt her moving in my direction. I was using my full weight and strength for leverage. I weighed 160 pounds. Suddenly, she gave way and fell back from the window ledge. She landed with all her weight right on top of me. She literally knocked the wind out of me.

At that moment, two aides who were responsible for the patients in X-ray, came into the room. They had lost track of her and paid no attention to me. They just grabbed her and led her away. I was groaning on the floor in agony. My supervisor walked in the office and said, "Whatever kind of weird therapy you're into now, I don't think this is the right place to practice it." She turned around and walked out. I still couldn't talk. Later, I told her the story, and she just nodded and said, "Oh."

## THE BASEMENTS OF BELLEVUE

One day Erwin and I decided to explore the basements of Bellevue. Erwin was a staff therapist, and I was his supervisor. The board of health gave us orders to take our ward cat back to the basements of Bellevue. Erwin and I got along fine. He was from Missouri and I was from Indiana. We felt a Midwestern kinship in the Big Apple. After hearing our accents, many people asked us if we were from Texas. We thought that was hilarious.

The first level of basements connected the Bellevue complex of hospitals underground. They were filled with pipes and hallways which seem to go everywhere and nowhere. There were always people walking through these basement corridors. Some were doctors, some were patients, and, as I found out later, some were homeless people looking for warmth. They all seemed to know where they were going.

The first level basement complex was also populated by hundreds of cats. Our ward kitty was about to return to her old stomping grounds. Erwin and I walked around looking for the corridor underneath the ward in hopes that she would stay there and protect us from mice and rats. To our surprise, the corridors ended in a brick wall and, at the center of this wall, was an old iron fire door. The door wouldn't open.

Erwin said there must be a million mice and rats behind the door. He thought we should find a way to get it open. We found an iron bar in a nearby closet and used it to open the door. To our surprise, we entered a lighted room. It was about twenty by fifteen feet and to our left we saw a stairway going down to another level. The stairs were old, but they seemed safe. The air was damp and moldy. We went down.

The next room was cold and made of old stone walls. It was illuminated by the light coming down the stairwell. Erwin pulled out a small flashlight. The room was empty; however, to our left again was another door. By this time

we were getting spooked. We figured we must be heading in the direction of the East River. The door was made out of old wood. It was not locked and just swung open on its hinges.

We were now in a long hallway. We couldn't see the end, and being Midwest boys we weren't about to go back. Down the hallway we walked. It was cold and dark and made from roughly cut stone. It seemed over a hundred years old. I had visions of finding skeletons. Erwin told me later that he was worried about being locked down there and being eaten by rats.

Just as we got to the end of the hallway, we saw another set of stairs leading further into the ground. Simultaneously, we saw the flicker of a flashlight coming up those stairs. Erwin said, "What the hell is that?" I didn't know what to say so I also said, "What the hell is that?"

Appearing before us was a man dressed in a silver aluminum foil suit. He looked like an astronaut coming from the bowels of the earth. His head was covered in a silver hood, and he had something that looked like a breathing tank strapped to his back.

He stopped in front of us and pulled off his silver hood. He said, "What are you boys doing down here?" I said in a weak voice trying to be official, "We're therapists and we're trying to find out why there are rats on our ward."

He said, "I wouldn't go no further. I'm the exterminator and it ain't safe down there."

Erwin said, "What's down there?"

He said, "Lots of river rats."

I said, "Well, I guess that answers our question. How far do these tunnels go anyway?"

He said, "I don't know."

That answer was good enough for Erwin and me. We were glad to have an excuse to leave. When we got back to the iron door, the exterminator locked it with a giant padlock. Then he said, "I wouldn't go down there again if I were you." He walked down the corridor and disappeared.

## NEW YORK DRAG RACES

My new office window overlooked the New York City morgue. The entrance to the morgue was on 30th Street, just off First Avenue, and sloped down towards the East River. Ambulances would back into the morgue loading dock and roll the bodies onto the platform where they would disappear into the bowels of New York Hospital.

On warm summer days, I would often sit and watch the bodies arrive, sort of a New York style meditation. Every now and then ambulance drivers would play games with the bodies. They would place the bodies, contained in a smooth vinyl body bag, on steel gurneys. Then they would line up two gurneys like cars at a drag race. The height of the loading dock exactly matched the height of the gurneys and the deck of the loading dock was smooth.

There was a slope at the entrance of the dock which provided an opportunity for the bodies to gain speed before hitting the loading dock wall. The drivers would let go of the bodies about twenty feet from the loading dock wall. It was quite a scene watching two corpses drag racing along 28th Street to their final destination. As they moved closer to the docks, the drivers would start cheering and rooting for their body.

When the gurneys hit the dock, the bodies would slide off onto the smooth platform, often for ten feet before coming to a stop. The drivers would run up the platform and measure which body had traveled the farthest. The winner would then collect his due.

## A NEW YORK PIANO CONCERT

Our therapy group voted to go to a free piano concert. Tom, a veteran of WWII suffered from hallucinations and an inability to concentrate. On this evening, however, the team decided it would be good for him to begin the process of leaving the hospital. The pianist was a young woman and there were about fifty people at the concert. The first half went very well. During the intermission the patients were all very happy and said how much they enjoyed the music. Because of their reaction, I had a false sense of relaxation. Usually I would always be on alert making sure everyone was OK. However, during the second half of the concert, I actually closed my eyes and began to enjoy the music.

Right at that moment, Tom began to cough. Everyone was looking. I had to make a decision and at the same time I was hoping Tom would just stop coughing. When a man sitting next to Tom asked him to be quiet, Tom went crazy. He looked at the man and then Tom began hitting his own head saying, in a loud voice right in the middle of *Claire de Lune*, "I got a steel plate in my head," over and over. Simultaneously, the rest of the patients were becoming more and more restless as Tom went on and on. I made my decision, gently grabbed Tom, and nudged him towards the lobby. He never stopped saying, "I got a steel plate in my head." When we got to the lobby I said, "Tom! Tom! I know you have a steel plate in your head and it's OK." He looked at me and said, "It is?" The young pianist just kept playing through all the commotion. She probably just thought this was normal for New York audiences.

## BELLEVUE CATS AND BELLEVUE RATS

We had a serious rat problem on one of our wards. Rats from the sub-basement had somehow found their way up to our ward. At night, they were running wild and biting patients in their beds. We decided to bring in some cats to solve the problem. An old timer on staff suggested we just go to the first level basement which connected the Bellevue complex of hospitals with tunnels. This was my third week on the job, and I hadn't yet realized there were tunnels underneath the hospital. I volunteered to go look for cats in the tunnels. The old timer said it would be easy and directed me to a staircase. The staircase seemed to go to nowhere, but to my surprise, I entered a large well-lit tunnel complex.

There were patients being wheeled around, people walking to different stairways and disappearing. There were groups of people standing around and talking. There were tunnels connecting to tunnels that seemed to go on and on. I started to walk, and to my surprise I began seeing cats. There were hundreds of cats throughout the tunnels. The cats were apparently allowed to stay and breed as a line of defense from mice and rats. I thought this was perfect. There is no doubt these cats know how to hunt rats. The problem I faced was that these were not "here kitty kitty" type cats. These were wild Bellevue cats.

The next day I bought a net and went cat hunting in the tunnels of Bellevue. I wore heavy gloves and eye protection. To this day, I am surprised that no one in the basements even gave me a second look as I walked along with eye goggles, thick gloves, a pole with a net, and a cat cage. I guess they had seen everything.

Within an hour, I caught and released four cats on our ward. The staff was excited and chipped in for cat boxes and some food. We all talked about how much we were supposed to feed them.

Within three days the rat bites stopped. We were all pleased. Within a month the cats were becoming more friendly. The patients were even finding the cats a valuable source of therapy. It is amazing how much feeling a cat can evoke from people. One woman who would not talk to us would talk to the cats for hours about her life. We were all in love with our Bellevue cats. Then one day, a man from the board of health came to visit our ward. He saw the cats and said, "These animals have to go. It's the law."

We told him about the rats and how we thought the cats were the lesser of two evils. We also told him that we thought the cats were good therapists for many patients. Unfortunately, he was a "rules are rules" type of guy. He just repeated himself, "I want these cats out of here by tomorrow. They are unsanitary."

I rounded up our kitties and took them back to the tunnels. Within a week our patients were suffering from rat bites. We called the man from the board of health and asked him what could be done. He suggested we put out rat poisoning. We said that rat poisoning was not such a good idea with psychiatric patients. We asked if he had other suggestions. He didn't.

## KITTY BELLEVUE

One day we decided that it was time to have a kitty. I suggested that I take a cat carrier and round up a cat in the basements of Bellevue Psychiatric Hospital. Everyone said, "What a great idea!" The next day I went to the pet shop and bought a cat carrier and went to the hospital basement with my son, Lars, who was 6 years old and very excited.

There were hundreds of cats in the basements of Bellevue. I just assumed they were friendly kitties since the maintenance staff always fed them. Lars got excited and went up to a kitty. The cats would run away and disappear into the pipes and walls.

After about two hours of roaming the basements with my 6-year-old, we came upon a black and white cat. He was sitting in a corner munching on some food. I thought he was about nine months to a year old. Lars said that he really liked him, so I went up to him very slowly. To my surprise, I was able to pick him up and put him in the cat carrier.

When we got to our loft, I let him go. He had everything a cat would want, including a cat box, scratch pole, bed, great food, and a small boy in love with him. We named him Kitty Bellevue. When we let him out of the container, he stretched and cautiously walked around.

It was at this point, I got a funny feeling. I could see clearly into Kitty Bellevue's eyes, and they were the eyes of a wild animal. This was a cat whose only human contact was occasional food from maintenance men or the well-meaning staff of Bellevue. Eventually, he went under the sink and huddled in a dark corner. We told Lars he needed to feel safe; however, we knew Kitty Bellevue might be a bit crazy.

That night we awoke to Kitty Bellevue yowling. The sound was like something out of a horror movie. I went into our kitchen room, and Kitty Bellevue was running full speed from one side of the room to another. Then I noticed that he had pooped and peed on the couch and two chairs. He looked at me with wild eyes, and before I could react he ran up me like a tree. From my shoulder, he jumped onto a shelf and proceeded to knock plates onto the floor.

Meanwhile, the pain from my flesh being used as a climbing tree was setting in very fast. I screamed and Kitty Bellevue got even wilder. I thought, "I'm going to get you!" I spent three hours tracking Kitty Bellevue. Finally, I cornered him in the shower and somehow got the cat container over his head.

I cleaned up my wounds and went to sleep for about two hours. I awoke to my son, Lars, saying, "Why is Kitty Bellevue back in his box?" After two hours of explaining to him why Kitty Bellevue was going back to the hospital, I was ready to commit myself. I called the hospital and took a sick day.

I took Kitty Bellevue back to the basements. Just as I let him go, my director happened to be walking through the same basement corridor. She said, "I thought you were sick. What are you doing here?"

I pointed to Kitty Bellevue and said, "That cat is crazy!"

She said, "Since when did we start doing therapy with cats."

I said, "It's a long story, and I need to go home and sleep."

She said OK and walked away. She never asked me again what I was doing in the basement on my sick day.

## STRAITJACKET

It was late at night, and I was really tired and ready to go home. Just as I was about to unlock the ward door, a man began screaming. The nurse and nurse's aide ran into the hallway and asked me to help. We found a recently admitted man huddled in the corner of the eating room. He was screaming and frantically moving his hands all over his body saying, "Get the bugs off! Get the bugs off!"

The nurse must have made a call because within three minutes, which seemed like three hours, four male aides appeared with a straitjacket. The man went really crazy, tried to run away and kept screaming about the bugs. These guys could have been on the front line for the New York Giants. They just grabbed him, put him on the floor, held him down, and within thirty seconds had him in a straitjacket.

There is something about being on the ward of a psychiatric hospital late at night with a man in a straitjacket screaming that he is covered with bugs. My adrenaline was pumping full force. The aides carried the man to a padded cell, placed him on the mats, and just walked away. I decided to stay. There was something about this man that bugged me, and I just couldn't bring myself to leave him alone. I went into the padded cell and sat on the mat next to him. He just kept rocking back and forth mumbling and sometimes screaming. After fifteen minutes, he leaned against me and began to cry. I held him.

I got home at 2 AM. It was a cold December night. The world seemed so empty and barren. I was exhausted. I looked at my son sleeping. He seemed so far away and so innocent. Somehow I managed to sleep.

## HERE COMES THE JUDGE

The Bellevue courtroom for in-hospital hearings was located on the seventh floor. One day several construction workers, without warning, began pounding on a wall. The patients became very agitated, so I asked them what they were doing. They said they were building a special bathroom for the judge. There was a staff bathroom ten feet from the judge's new bathroom that was hardly used. I told the construction workers, and they told us that the judge needed his own bathroom. They just kept pounding away. They finished the judge's bathroom in four weeks. Normal construction workers would have finished in four days. Because there was little space to work with, it turned out to be very small.

The judge weighed over three hundred pounds and always wore his robes. I guess he was determined to use his bathroom which had a sign on the front which read Judge. He made a court recess and walked to his private bath-room. He somehow managed to squeeze in. After twenty minutes, we began to wonder if the judge had constipation or diarrhea. Then, we heard a knocking coming from his closed door.

The judge was stuck. He couldn't get past the door. We all were doing everything we could not to laugh out loud. The patients kept talking about payback. After two hours, the construction guys showed up. They removed the door, and the judge managed to slip out. Later, I found out that the judge's bathroom cost the city of New York $15,000. In my opinion, it was worth it because we kept telling the story for weeks, and the patients were very happy.

## JUMPER

Bill was young, athletic, and energetic. When I met Bill on the ward, all he could talk about was women. No one knew for sure what was troubling Bill. He signed himself into the hospital for evaluation. Today, I suspect that he suffered from bipolar disorder or what used to be known as manic-depression.

Our psychiatric team decided that Bill should be allowed to go hiking. I lead the hiking group to Bear Mountain, and as we walked up the mountain Bill and I talked. He talked about women at first and how he needed to take cold showers all the time. Then he talked about fast cars and wanting to be a race car driver.

When we got to the top of the mountain, something changed in Bill. He seemed calm and unusually clear.

We just sat in silence for about five minutes. Five minutes of silence with Bill was like five days with a normal person. When I looked at Bill, his eyes looked tired, and he said, "I love life." Something about the way he said it struck a chord deep in my being. I felt chills go up my spine. It was as though Bill was giving me a special gift on top of the mountain.

Two weeks later I was called to Bill's SRO (Single Room Residency) on 30th Street between Third and Lexington. Apparently he was acting strange and had asked for me. As I walked around the corner, I was overcome by the flashing red lights of police cars and fire trucks. A few moments later, I saw Bill's body on top of a car. He had jumped from the seventh story and landed on the roof of a parked car.

I told the police who I was, and they let me come closer. I held the moment on the mountain in my mind as I identified Bill.

## RIDING THE STATEN ISLAND FERRY

One of my favorite places to do therapy was on the Staten Island Ferry. In those days the ferry ride, which went from Battery Park at the southern tip of Manhattan Island to Staten Island, cost 10 cents. I would leave the ward with a group of patients, and we would walk to the IRT 6 Subway and take it downtown to Battery Park. We would then walk over to the ferry terminal and wait.

Once we were on the ferry, the fun began. There was always a fresh ocean breeze coming in from the Atlantic Ocean via the Verrazano Narrows Bridge. Each side of the ferry had a different view. From one side, we could see the Verrazano Bridge. From the other side, we could see Ellis Island, the Statue of Liberty, up the Hudson River, and parts of Manhattan. From the back of the ferry we could see the white water of the wake and the many skyscrapers of southern Manhattan, including the World Trade Center. On a good night, we could see the Empire State Building. From the front of the ferry, we could see Staten Island approaching, and there was a sense of vast openness as we slipped between the Statue of Liberty and the Verrazano Bridge.

Inside the ferry we could sit, relax, read, talk, and have a snack at the snack bar. Sometimes classical musicians would set up and play string quartets. For me, every place on the boat was magical. Each area had a different quality. Whenever I had a difficult day or I needed to calm down, I would ride the ferry before going home. I felt the wind hit my face and the fresh air filled with negative ions and it was like a deep cleansing. I remember a night when I was so pumped with adrenaline that I thought I would never come down. I sat on the Verrazano side of the ferry and took deep breaths for over fifteen minutes. On the way back, I went to the front of the boat and just watched Manhattan getting closer and closer.

When I began the trip, my mind was racing and my body was jumping. When I returned, I had a new perspective on life. My body was calm, and my mind was centered. I walked from the ferry to my loft in Tribeca. Seeing the moon shining down onto the streets between the skyscrapers calmed me and I slept well that night.

When I took patients to the ferry, we would stay together as a group. There would always be one nurses' aide and/or activity therapist who would assist me. This gave me the freedom to talk with different members of the group. For example, the assistant may have sat with the group inside listening to classical music, while I sat outside with a patient talking about his life. In this sense, the whole ferry became my office, and I would choose what part of the ferry was best for different conversations. I talked with hundreds of patients on the Staten Island Ferry. Something about being on the water in the open air facilitated meaningful conversations.

Ted was 30 years old and very depressed. He didn't want to leave the ward. I told him we would be going on the Staten Island Ferry, and that I would be with him. After several minutes, Ted said he wanted to go; however, he wanted to be by my side. I agreed, and we all headed out for our evening adventure. Once you leave the ward with a group of patients, unknown adventures become very real. You know that anything is possible.

On this evening, all went smoothly as the ferry left Battery Park with its deep whistles as the motors churned the dark waters into a bubbling white wake. Ted and I sat together at the rear of the boat. After about five minutes Ted said, "John, I have so many things going on. I feel lost." Then he started to cry. I let Ted lean on me, and I put my arm around him. We sat in silence for a few minutes, and when I looked up, I saw the tall buildings of Manhattan look like tinker toys with lights.

I believe Ted and I came to the same place at the same time. He sat up and said, "John, it's all so little."

I said, "This is a new perspective. Your problems are even smaller."

Ted said, "Yes."

I said, "Ted, what will you do?"

He replied, "I am going to work hard. I know I can make it."

The conversation was so simple. Underneath the words and in the gestalt of the ferry, I felt a special energy. Ted had come to a realization, and so had I. At that moment, I felt as though Ted and I were both touched by the same energy. I knew that I was also going to make it, and that life was a very special gift.

The next day on the ward, Ted looked different. He told Dr. S that he was ready to go home. Home for Ted was an SRO (Single Residency Occupancy). He was discharged the next day. When I visited Ted four weeks later, he was working for a magazine and making money on his own. I got caught up in my hospital duties and lost track of Ted.

Four years after I left Bellevue, I was going through a divorce. My life was a mess. I went to the ferry, sat down, and began to cry. After about five minutes of sitting there with my head in my hands, I noticed a man sitting next to me. He said, "It's all right, John" and put his arms around my shoulders. I felt an immense security when I realized it was Ted. I was sitting in the same place we were in four years before.

I said, "Thank you, Ted" and asked him what was he doing here. He said that he came to this spot on the ferry at least once a week. He said the spot for him was a source of renewal. A week later, I had dinner with Ted and his fiancé at his new apartment.

## CELIA AND TOMMY

When I worked at Bellevue Psychiatric Hospital, two of my patients, Celia and Tommy, devised unique head devices to protect them from receiving different frequencies through their cranium. These were made from hanger wires, pieces of cans, and aluminum foil. Every day they searched the streets for new pieces of foil and tin to maximize their protection.

I spent a good amount of time trying to understand Celia and Tommy who were, in their own way, very intelligent people. Tommy had a college degree in mathematics, and Celia had two years of art school. They were New York "street people," acting crazy only when they needed to check into the hospital for a good meal. Other than that, they were able to fend for themselves.

I asked them why they wore their special head protectors. Tommy told me that one day he began hearing voices and couldn't tune them out. He said they were both sensitive to different frequencies. He told me his theory about increased radio waves. He said how our head was like a crystal oscillator in a radio, and functioned like a receiver for these waves. His head gear helped him block out or dull these frequencies and voices.

One day, I asked Celia if I could remove a piece of foil from her head protector. She agreed, but only for a few moments. I removed a small piece of aluminum foil. Her face changed drastically, and she began to talk in fast gibberish. Tommy got upset. He understood what she was saying. I immediately put the foil back in place. Celia's face relaxed. She couldn't remember what had just happened.

That evening, I kept thinking about my experience with Celia. Her speaking reminded me of my boyhood experiences listening to the local church group of the Pentecostals "speaking in tongues." I began to wonder if Tommy and Celia were tuned into similar voices. Maybe the voices and frequencies they perceived were real. Maybe their cranial devices really did do something. My thoughts about Tommy and Celia always seemed like forbidden territory for a therapist. I felt like I was going over the edge of established therapy. At that time, I didn't share my thoughts with my peers at Bellevue. I kept them to myself for fear of being misunderstood.

In the days of old, royalty crowns were head devices made from precious metals and stones. Some people thought that the Kings and Queens who wore these crowns were gifted with divine blood and were able to receive divine messages from Spirits. The precious metals and stones of their crowns served as amplification devices for receiving divine guidance for their kingdoms. Tommy and Celia wore their "crowns" to block out frequencies while the Kings and Queens wore their crowns to receive messages.

In 1975, I met an osteopath from England who explained to me that the bones of the cranium were mobile. He told me that a branch of Osteopathic medicine known as Cranial Osteopathy was devoted only to the cranium. He said the founder, Dr. William Garner Sutherland, invented a head device to prove his theory of cranial bone mobility. The device was made to fit over the cranium with a system of screws which was used to apply systematic pressure to the different cranial bones. By experimenting with himself, he proved that restriction of cranial bone mobility would produce symptoms like headaches, body aches and pains, changes in thinking and emotion, and could possibly be the source of different diseases.

When he told me the story of Dr. Sutherland and his cranial device, I couldn't help but remember my experiences with Tommy and Celia. I later learned that towards the end of his career, Dr. Sutherland gave lectures on liquid light, waves of energy passing through our cranium, and frequency transmissions. I began to think Tommy and Celia were intuitively aware of something which Dr. Sutherland had been investigating from a very different perspective.

## PIZZA

Our leisure group decided to go to Rockies Pizza Parlor for dinner. Rockies was located on Second Avenue and 28th Street by the hospital. There were seven of us: five patients, a nurse who wanted pizza and volunteered to go, and myself. We sat in the back of the restaurant and ordered three large pizzas. One of my patients, Jose, was acting strange. He kept erratically jerking his head while talking to his silverware. I was wondering if he left the hospital too early or had somehow not taken his medication.

The pizza parlor was empty except for a man who was very obese sitting at a table eating an extra large pizza. This man must have weighed over four hundred pounds. It was a struggle for him to sit close enough to the table to reach his pizza. His belly served as a secondary table. Jose kept looking at him. He would stare at him, twitch, and then talk to his silverware. The nurse and I kept trying to distract Jose and carry on a conversation with the other patients. Jose would have no part of it. He was fixated on the obese man.

We were about halfway through our pizzas when Jose jumped up. He screamed and ran over to the man. He said something to him in gibberish, picked up the man's pizza, and threw it all over him. Jose then began running around his table screaming and waving his arms. Jose just went faster and faster and the man just sat there with pizza dripping off his face.

All this took place in less than a minute. I jumped up, ran to Jose, and tried to grab him. Jose was pumped up and I just spun away from him. I screamed, "Jose, stop this right now!" Jose looked into my eyes. His eyes were both vacant and wild. Jose wasn't home. He turned and ran out of the pizza parlor turning over every table as he left. I ran after him. I watched him run down Second Avenue at full speed screaming and swinging his arms. The funny thing about it was that no one but me seemed to notice. Everyone he passed just kept walking and going about their business. I ran to the corner, but Jose was gone.

When I walked back to the pizza place, I found the nurse trying to explain to the manager, who spoke little English, what had happened. The patients were sitting at their table eating pizza as though nothing had happened. The man hadn't moved—he was just sitting there in shock. I got a wet wash cloth and some napkins and began helping him clean up. He finally said, "What happened?"

I told him I was a therapist and that something must have been off with the patient's medication. He looked at me and said, "That's OK, I understand." Then he got up, still covered with pizza, walked over to the nurse and manager, and paid for himself and our group. I thanked him and he said, "That's OK. This was a sign from God that I should begin my diet today."

## NEW YORK BUREAUCRACY

We needed money. I asked Jane, my director, when I would get my two year raise as stated in my contract. We were in the process of rolling back our NYU grant from the City of New York. Everyone was afraid of salary cuts, poor management, and lack of support for patient care. As it turned out, our fears were mostly true.

Jane handed me my paycheck envelope and said, "Take a look and see if it's there." I opened the envelope, and my eyes nearly came out of my head. I expected to see a check for $523 after taxes and was hoping to see a check for $605 with my raise. Instead the check was for $856.50. I looked at Jane and said, "What is this?" She handed me another envelope and said maybe this would explain. I opened it and there was another check for $856.50 from the City of New York. I thought, "Uh oh!" And Jane said, "Good luck."

I found my way to the payroll office. I was afraid to cash the checks. I thought the city would sue me or put me in jail. I remember waiting over an hour to see someone. Finally, I went into her office and showed her the checks. She looked at them and screamed, "Why are you showing me these checks? Don't you know that to change these would be very bad? Everything is really messed up. Don't worry, it'll be all right. Now get out and don't come back!"

I left. Later that day I cashed the checks. I kept thinking that the New York City bureaucracy would catch this, but instead they kept giving me paychecks for $856.50. I never went back to the payroll office.

## A GOOD NIGHTS SLEEP

We took the children from the ward to the Frost Valley YMCA camp in the Catskills for a nature adventure. They were having a great time swimming and playing in the woods. I remember thinking that this was great. What a wonderful experience this would be for these disturbed inner-city children.

That evening we had a campfire and told stories. They were "happy campers." We all went back to our cabins and made sure the kids were safely in bed. I woke up at 1 AM to the sound of children talking. I asked them what was going on. I thought they were probably excited and couldn't sleep.

They said they were afraid. I thought maybe they were afraid of a bear or of wild animals. One of the campfire skits involved bears in the woods. They said, "It's all those noises."

I thought, "What can they be talking about. There are no car horns or sirens out here. It's so quiet and still."

At that moment, the camp counselor came into the cabin carrying a ghetto blaster. He said, "Don't worry, everything will be all right." At the sight of the ghetto blaster the children visibly relaxed. He put it on a table and turned it on. Suddenly, I heard the sounds of cars, buses, motorcycles, and sirens that the counselor had recorded in New York City. The children were asleep within five minutes. The camp counselor looked at me and said, "It never fails."

## PARANOID WOOD CHOPPING

We decided to do a pilot study on the effects of overnight camping on adult psychiatric patients. On our overnight camping trip, every patient helped. They cooked, cleared the campsite, set up the tent, and washed the dishes. I was sitting against a rock enjoying myself and taking a moment's rest. The campfire was burning, and the smell of dinner was in the air. I was drifting away when Margaret said that we needed more wood for the fire. I was half asleep and somewhat overcome by the fresh mountain air. In other words, I wasn't as alert as I should have been.

I said, "OK," and out of the corner of my eye I saw Ed. I said, "Ed, get that ax over there and chop up some fire wood."

Ed got a great big smile and something inside of me said, "I have never seen anyone that happy over chopping wood." Then I drifted off to sleep.

Suddenly my eyes popped open, and I jumped up. What was I doing giving Ed of all people an ax? Ed was paranoid and prone to fits of violence. I looked around expecting to see people chopped up. Instead, I saw Ed sitting by the fire with the women. The ax was next to the woodpile. I took a deep breath and was happy to be alive. I kept a very close watch over the ax for the rest of the camping trip.

## BEAR MOUNTAIN

Our leisure group voted to take the ferry to Bear Mountain Park and climb Bear Mountain. The ferry ride from Manhattan to Bear Mountain was wonderful. It was a sunny July day. The patients were relaxed and calm. For several, it was the first time they had been out of New York City. They were excited. In general, everyone was getting along, talking, and having a good time.

When we arrived at Bear Mountain, we had lunch together and began to start up the mountain. We mostly walked up in silence. Sometimes I would stop to show them different trees, animal foot prints, or insects. They were like little kids.

When we reached the top, there was a large rock perfect for sitting. It was very warm from the sun, and we were all very quiet between the silence of the mountain top and the warmth of the rock. At least this is what happened to me.

I asked the patients to tune into the mountain silence compared to the sounds of New York City. We all sat in a circle and it became very still. I thought, "This must be something for them." When the silence felt profound, Florence spoke up.

Florence was a wonderful woman. She grew up in Harlem and suffered from depression. She was about 51 old and a hospital regular. Florence was very excited about the trip to Bear Mountain. She said that when she was a little girl her parents took her there once.

Right in the middle of the silence, Florence said in a very loud voice, "What did you say? What did you say?" Apparently Florence wore a hearing aid, which I did not know about. Something had malfunctioned. I said, "Florence, relax and enjoy the silence. It's much different here than the city."

She said, "What did you say? What did you say?"

Meanwhile, the other patients were still meditating on the silence as though Florence was not speaking. It was clear they wanted to please me. The louder Florence became, the more they went into their own worlds.

Finally I got right in Florence's ear and screamed, "Don't worry, Florence, everything is all right."

She looked at me with her big eyes, started to laugh ,and said, "Thank you, Dr. John. You're such a nice man."

Meanwhile, the other patients took this as a signal to share their experiences of silence. No one spoke of Florence screaming. We walked down the mountain. Every so often I would yell in Florence's ear. The other patients just accepted it as normal communication and went on about their business.

## A LITTLE PUSH

The patients were in the music therapy room and waiting for their session. Chuck, the music therapist, was sitting outside the room staring at the wall. He looked like many of the patients waiting for their sessions. The ward nurse called me because she thought Chuck needed help.

I walked up to Chuck and asked, "What's going on?"

He looked at the floor and seemed unresponsive. This wasn't like Chuck. So I put my arm around him and tried again, "Chuck, what's going on? Talk to me."

Chuck mumbled, "My partner broke up with me. I can't go on."

I said, "I am sorry and we can talk about it later. Right now you have a session, and there are patients waiting for you."

Chuck looked at the floor and said, "I can't."

I said, "Look, Chuck, it will take your mind off your partner. It could be like therapy for you. You have to learn how to take these things one step at a time."

I literally lifted Chuck up and placed him in front of the swinging doors to the session room. He kept saying, "I can't. I just can't."

I don't know what came over me, but somehow I just knew Chuck needed to be in the session room. Call it a gut feeling. I gave Chuck a strong push, and to my surprise he went spinning through the doors into the session room. Just as I thought he was going to fall down, he caught himself, jumped up, and with a big smile said, "Hi, everyone, let's make music!"

The patients, who were a few seconds before in a similar state as Chuck, started clapping. Chuck went to work.

That evening Chuck came to my office. He said the music therapy session he did that afternoon was the best session of his life. Now he had a better perspective. He thanked me for pushing him through the door and said that was a very unusual supervision method. He didn't remember that course in the university.

I told him when we give a session, we get a session.

## A GREAT CONCERT

Susan was 27 years old and very troubled. She had been repeatedly abused by her stepfather and many men in her life. From time to time, she would become clinically depressed. We were sitting at the piano. I asked Susan to play something. She liked music and had never played the piano. I told her just to enjoy the sounds and let whatever happen, happen. She began to touch notes. I responded. The goal of the therapy was to relate through music rather than words.

Susan played more, and I responded with more music. Suddenly Susan changed. She began pounding the keys in anger. I pounded in an echo. This went on for over five minutes. Then she changed to a high-pitched note and played it softly over and over. The emotion in that one note was as powerful as the greatest emotional performance of any concert pianist.

She continued to play the same note over and over for ten minutes. I closed my eyes and listened. The variations and texture of sound were stunning. Then there came a silence, a deep fertile silence. Without warning, she screamed. I instinctually grabbed her, and she began to cry. She cried for several minutes. Then she told me her life dreams. She wanted to write poetry, meet a loving man, and have children.

We didn't talk about her abuse. We communicated on a deep level through music. We were beyond words. Susan's life dreams were the closest words to express her feelings at that moment. When our session was over, Susan went back to the ward. Her eyes were bright, and she thanked me. I thanked her. Although I was the therapist, something profound had changed in my life. I felt more open and alive to the world. I got in touch with my own dreams. Susan's music was inspiring and to this day was one of the greatest concerts I had ever heard.

I saw Susan five years later walking down the streets of the West Village. She recognized me before I saw her, and called out my name. She looked good. She said her life was sometimes crazy and that she was writing poetry. When our eyes met, we both recognized and reconfirmed the power of our "therapeutic encounter" in the hospital. No words were spoken. I took a deep breath, and we said goodbye.

## THE BOWERY

One day I was called to a flop house in the Bowery. We were trying to extend our services into the community and help people before they reached the hospitalization stage. I walked into a small dirty room that smelled of human waste and where cockroaches darted from wall to wall. There was a man lying on a filthy bed covered with spit and vomit. A priest sat next to him preparing to give him his last rites.

I felt disgusted and angry with this man for letting his life fall to such a low level. My judgmental thoughts were spinning out of control. I kept saying to myself, "John, you are a professional, and you have seen this before." Another voice kept saying, "How disgusting. What a horrible person. How low can a human being go?"

I wanted to walk out, but for some unknown reason I stayed. As the priest gave the last rites, the man opened his eyes and said, "I see Jesus." He began to glow—it was as if a light surrounded him. As this happened, the energy in the room dramatically changed. I watched this dirty, dying man whom I had cast judgment on, transform into a radiant being. His glowing energy enveloped the room. I felt as though I was being blessed and showered with grace.

Without warning, the man sat up and said, "Do you see him? Do you see him? He is coming." He exhaled his last breath and fell back onto the bed. His dying process lasted only a few minutes, which seemed like an eternity. I looked at his body on the bed and touched his hand. I realized that I was crying for the loss of the most important spiritual teachers of my life.

## SHOWER THERAPY

Sue, the assistant director, invited me to share an office with her on the sixth floor. Since I worked from 2 PM to 10 PM and Sue worked from 8 AM to 5 PM, we were rarely in the office at the same time. It was perfect.

I remember sitting in the office looking out at the East River and allowing my thoughts to unwind. In the chaos of Bellevue, I found a special, quiet place. Sometimes there are just no answers even though you are hoping for some to appear. Sometimes I would sit and my mind would be running at high speed trying to find a way to help a patient. Other times I would sit and my body would be surging with adrenaline. It would be an effort just to stay in the chair.

Then one day Sue came into the office and said, "Did you know we have our own shower?"

I said, "Why would anyone put a shower in an office. Does it work?"

Sue said, "This used to be part of an old ward. When they converted it to an office, they just left the shower. It still works."

I laughed and said, "Well, at least we can be clean therapists."

Sue showed me the shower behind a closet and left.

The next evening a patient attempted suicide and I was the first on the scene. She had tried to cut her wrists and failed. There was blood everywhere but not enough to indicate she had hit her radial artery. Nevertheless, my adrenals switched on and I went on high alert. I checked her out and carried her into the main room where the nurses took over.

When I got back to my office, my emotions were racing. I tried to sit in my chair and look out over the river. I couldn't hold still. I began pacing the floor and taking deep breaths. Then I remembered what Sue had shown me the day before.

I pulled back the clothes in the closet, took off my clothes, and got into the shower. I turned on the water and let it get nice and hot. I stood in the shower for a long time. At the end, I switched to ice cold water. It felt great. I screamed and took deep breaths.

When I got out of the shower, I went to my seat and looked out over the East River. Everything was moving slower. I could actually sit.

I used that shower many times. I will never laugh again at the idea of a shower in an office.

## BEING STALKED

Bellevue could be an intense work environment in many ways. I supervised the children's ward which was staffed by two activity therapists and three aides. One of the aides was slacking off and I was asked by my director to check him out.

I soon discovered that "checking out" was like being a detective. During supervision I told him his work times and what I expected him to do. I had to document the times and assignments and have him read and sign the paper. He took the paper to his union and signed it two weeks later.

Meanwhile, I began observing and documenting his work behaviors in reference to his work agreement. Over a period of three months, he missed over fifty hours of patient time and left on the average of one hour early every work day. When he did work, he just sat and looked out the window rather than interacting with the children. Two nurses, the other aides and activity therapists, and the ward doctor and I participated in the documentation of his work behavior.

I presented the findings to my director and she said, "Fire him!" I had no idea how to "fire" someone. I thought the documentation of behavior was enough to bring him before a disciplinary committee. However, little did I know that this had already taken place two times before I was hired. Now, in a matter of seconds, I was told to fire someone.

I went into shock. Although the man was slacking off and had problems, the therapist in me wanted to help him. He was clearly depressed. However, on a work level his time was up. My job was to let him go. All the documentation was to prepare the hospital administration for any union confrontations which were sure to come. I was the one who had to sit him down, give him his notice, and see him every day for two weeks before he left. I felt like a pawn of the hospital administration having to do the dirty work.

I sat him down and told him. He didn't take it well. During the meeting he threatened my life. He said, "You betrayed me, and I will get you when you least expect it."

I thought, "This is a hospital, and he is a man responsible for working with children. If he is threatening me, there is no doubt he needs to leave." I stood up, looked down at him and said in a firm voice, "You're welcome to come after me, but you better make it good. I leave the hospital in the evenings at 9 PM and walk to the subway. I look forward to our meeting." I was angry and did not like being threatened.

He said, "You better not turn your back," implying that he knew how to use a knife.

I thought, "This wasn't covered during my graduate training." Then I said, "You better know what you're doing."

He stormed out of my office.

I told my director and the chief hospital administrator what had happened. I did not receive any support from them. In typical bureaucratic style, they just disappeared. I was on my own with this one. For four weeks, I felt the tension of being stalked. I understand how women and celebrities feel when they are being stalked.

I got word after four weeks that he had moved and was no longer in the city. I felt an immense wave of relief. Everyone said, "John, you look so much more relaxed." They didn't know what was happening. I knew that something had changed in me forever. A level of innocence was gone. I was stronger and at the same time more weary and hardened.

## CAKE AND COFFEE

I never understood the logic of giving insane and depressed people lots of sugar and coffee. However, anyone who has ever worked in these facilities knows that the patients are encouraged to eat lots of candy, given as much coffee as they can drink, and encouraged to smoke cigarettes. I remember patients hanging around the door waiting for our snack cart. Some would be walking around in circles mumbling and smoking. Others would be sitting and staring at the ceiling. This was an everyday occurrence. I always wanted to create an environment that would help patients to develop better living habits. I created a camping program, and it was amazing the changes we saw in two days.

## A GREAT SHOW

Many of my patients became "crazy" as winter set in. They were great actors who were homeless and needed a place to stay for the winter. They could fool the best psychiatrists and therapists.

One of my patients had years of training as an actor and had performed in many Broadway productions. One day I said to him, "Henry, why is it that you always come here for help in February?"

He said in a serious tone, "John, it's cold out there."

I said, "Look, Henry, I'm not your psychiatrist. I won't say anything, so it would make my job easier if you could play a normal part."

Henry looked at me and said, "Do you want me to play a normal person?"

I said, "Well, Henry, not too normal—that would be boring."

Henry said, "I understand."

Henry and I got along just fine. Every now and then he would have an episode on the ward. One day after he had an episode, Henry said to me, "Too bad you missed that one. Everyone applauded."

# BELLEVUE
# IS EVERYWHERE

I WAS WALKING HOME from Bellevue through New York's East Village with Chuck, my friend and colleague. It was Friday night. We had a challenging week of work at Bellevue Psychiatric Hospital, and we were tired.

Chuck said, "It is sure good to get away from the hospital."

I agreed, "You can take just so much craziness in one day."

Then it suddenly dawned on Chuck and me that we were walking past many of our patients. They were sitting on the sidewalk and leaning against buildings.

I said, "Chuck, are you seeing what I am seeing?"

From 14th Street to the Bowery, we counted seventeen patients. Most were just staring into space or talking to themselves. However, two patients recognized us and said hello.

Chuck said, "Our patients are everywhere," in an understated way.

Sure enough, it wasn't just our patients but many others we didn't know. They were talking to themselves, staring into space, and acting bizarre. On the corner of First Avenue and Houston Street, a bearded man with wild eyes pushed a cart filled with garbage screaming, "They Are Here! They Are Here!"

A young woman walked past us crying hysterically. When she began to cross the street against the light, a taxi driver honked at her and screamed profanities at her. She never looked up and continued to walk through traffic.

A chilling thought came to me at that moment: The line between sanity and insanity is a continuum that we all travel every day. If we stay too long at the extreme of the insane end, we may end up in Bellevue. If we stay too long at the extreme of the sane end, our life will become rigid, dull, and boring.

I always said that the only difference between my patients and me was that I had the key to the hospital and they didn't. On that day, my words rang true. The walls of Bellevue were clearly not as solid as I thought. Chuck and I both acknowledged feeling like we were still on the ward, and yet we were in the middle of New York City, in a supposedly sane environment.

At every moment, we are all constantly moving along a continuum of sanity and insanity. When I worked at Bellevue, I met a surgeon when I was having lunch at the cafeteria. He was in hospital greens with his stethoscope hanging around his neck. We talked about golf and basketball for about fifteen minutes until his beeper went off and he disappeared.

Three months later, I was walking home through the Bowery. A man sitting on the sidewalk leaning against an abandoned building caught my eye. He was dirty, unshaven, and smelled of alcohol and urine. He wasn't aware that I was looking at him. I began to walk down the street when I realized he was the surgeon with whom I had had lunch with! For a moment, it was like the tale "The Emperor's New Clothes." I couldn't believe it. One day he was a doctor performing surgery, the next day he was a drunk living on the streets of New York City!

I went back and sat next to him and said, "Have you played any golf lately?"

He said, "I need some coffee."

We went to a Bowery coffee shop and talked. He told me that coming to the Bowery, getting drunk, and being crazy was his way of unwinding from the hospital and the pressures of surgery. He asked me what I did to unwind. I told him I took cold showers, walked home, played the piano, and meditated. He took a drink of coffee and said, "I wish they would build a golf course in Manhattan."

I asked him if he would be OK.

He said, "I do this every month. It's my therapy."

I never saw him again. I have heard that he is a well-known surgeon and sought after by many people around the world.

There is a *Star Trek* episode where a very orderly and peaceful society went totally mad once a month. They planned for and made their crazy time a special event. When the time was over, they went back to being passive, ordered, and peaceful.

I have come to believe that the difference between sanity and insanity is our ability to remember and act upon the rules of society. When we do something repeatedly that is out of alignment with the rules of society, people around us become threatened and/or become a threat to themselves (suicidal behavior). It is interesting to note that these rules change from place to place as well as from time to time.

When I worked at Richmond State Psychiatric Hospital, we admitted two gay men based on their homosexuality as a psychiatric disorder. Three years later I was working at Bellevue and the American Psychiatric Association determined that homosexuality was not a psychiatric disorder. The gay doctors, nurses, and therapists threw a party to celebrate their sanity.

One of my patients at Bellevue came up with the most bizarre stories. He would spend hours in the work program office telling us about alligators in the sewers or how the radio towers on the World Trade Center were for communications with alien beings. I remember times when up to ten staff members would sit and listen to his stories.

One day, someone got the idea that he should be a reporter for the *National Enquirer*. A nurse said that she knew someone who could get him an interview. We spent hours teaching him how to dress and talk for his interview. He came back and said the interview took five hours and during that time he told stories. Two weeks later he was hired and went on to become a very successful reporter. You may have read his stories while buying groceries.

In the early days of the thirteen colonies people who acted bizarre were given the name *lunatic*. This was because people noticed that their bizarre behaviors tended to increase during full moon cycles. These people were normally kept hidden by their families and were sometimes tied up or locked in their rooms. When the families got tired of caring for them, they just took them out onto the road and let them go. They would then wander from town to town.

In those days it was believed that their bizarre behavior was the work of the devil or evil spirits. It was called bestiality. This meant that the person was behaving outside the rules of society and had regressed to a state of animal behavior and/or was possessed by a demon. One treatment was to tie and shackle them in a basement without food. Of course, these patients would howl from cold and lack of food, which was further proof of their animalistic behavior.

If that didn't work, there was the method of bloodletting, which would be an attempt to get the bad blood out that was filled with the evil spirits. If the patient died, it was for the best, and they were pronounced cured.

I was in the recreation room at Richmond State Psychiatric Hospital looking for some board games for the patients. One game had fallen from the shelf and lodged itself between the shelf and the wall. I pushed on the box and tried to slide it up between the shelf and the wall. To my surprise, the wall gave way where I was pushing. I got a flashlight and could see there was clearly a walled-up room behind the shelves.

I spent twenty minutes clearing off the shelves and moving them out of the way. Then with a hammer, I began chipping away at the wall. It was old and mostly crumbled. Behind the wall, I discovered a room with old stone walls and a dirt floor. The room was about fifteen feet deep and eight feet wide. Along the walls were sets of iron shackles.

Chills ran along my spine as I realized this was an old therapy room. The hospital was over 80 years old, and the room was used to shackle patients a long time ago. When the hospital administrator heard about my discovery, the administration had the shackles removed and the room closed with a concrete cinder block wall. I was told to forget about my discovery.

Although we have stopped shackling and beating patients, much of the same mentality still exists. I worked

with patients who had had frontal lobotomies. In this procedure, a probe is inserted up the nose into the frontal
lobe of the brain and brain tissue is snipped away. These
patients were quite docile and had lost all ability to relate
to people. I worked with patients who had received over
a hundred electroshock treatments. They were, in many
cases, walking vegetables.

I called him "beep-beep" man. The beep-beep man was
committed to the hospital ten years before as a criminal
sexual psychopath. I read his file and found out that he had
been electroshocked 322 times in 10 years. All the beep-
beep man could do was shuffle in circles, rub his fingers
together for a cigarette, sometimes mumble, and make a
sound like beep-beep.

While I was working at Bellevue, the comptroller for
the City of New York released a study stating that up to
60 percent of America's mental patients were walking the
streets of New York City. The purpose of the report was
to get more federal funding for halfway houses and mental
health facilities. However, the idea of 60 percent of our
nation's mental patients walking on the streets of New York
City was something to contemplate.

Most New Yorkers I spoke with would say things like,
"It's good someone said it."

"I think the number is too low."

"They should include Miami in the winter as part of
New York."

"I know a lot of people in my neighborhood who were left out."

The movie *Men in Black* is about aliens from outer space living on planet Earth. The aliens can all disguise themselves to look like normal human beings. No one knows about them except for a special group of people called the *Men in Black*. There is a line where a *Man in Black* detective tells his partner, a new man in black detective, that two-thirds of the aliens who live on planet Earth are located in New York City. His partner thinks for a moment and says, "Are most of them cab drivers?"

When working in a psychiatric setting you gain a new perspective on life. You become aware of behaviors that you might not have noticed before in the course of a normal day. There is, in fact, no such thing as a normal day at Bellevue.

The difference between the New York subways and Bellevue Psychiatric, as far as I can tell, is a matter of location.

One morning while riding the subway, a man who was well dressed in an expensive suit and tie was pacing back and forth talking to someone who was not there.

"He kept saying, "No! No! No! You had better listen. Of course not. Maybe tomorrow," etc., etc., etc.

Another man entered the subway car selling, of all things, porno movies. He was waving titles like *Naughty Cheerleaders*, *Deep Penetration*, and *Housewife Lust* screaming, "Get them here at a bargain!"

To my surprise several men were actually looking over the titles and thinking about buying some tapes as he moved through the car. When he came to the man in the suit, he held up a porno video in front of his face. The man just kept talking. For some reason, the porno movie vendor thought it was necessary to convince him to buy the movie. He went into graphic detail about the sex in the movie in a very loud voice.

The man in the suit just kept talking. I looked around the subway which was mostly filled with people on their way to work. They were reading papers, looking at billboard advertising, or sleeping. I was reminded of my days on the psychiatric ward when one patient would act bizarre and the other patients would stare into space as though nothing was happening. Once again, I had the feeling that I was back in the hospital and that Bellevue Was Everywhere.

When I left Bellevue Psychiatric, my fellow therapists gave me a special gift. They took the master key to the wards of Bellevue and encased it in plastic. The key is like no other key. It is about 6 inches long, made of solid steel, weighs several ounces, and has the look of something that could open an old vault. Everyone joked and told me that, just in case I found myself in a difficult spot, I might need the key. They said that I had earned it.

# ACKNOWLEDGEMENTS

I want to acknowledge the staff of Bellevue Psychiatric Hospital, Richmond State Psychiatric Hospital, and Central State Psychiatric Hospital.

I especially want to acknowledge:

My wife, Thea Keats Beaulieu, for feedback and editing

My sons: Lars and twins Daniel and Lucas
and my granddaughter Lua,
for being who they are

Pamela Kersage, who knows these stories and
for the creative design of this book

Professor Arnold Johnson, Purdue University

Professor Carol Ann Peterson, Indiana University

John Parrish, Ph.D., Psychologist,
Richmond State Psychiatric Hospital

Ron Mullens, Activity Therapist,
Richmond State Psychiatric Hospital

Mike Jordon, Activity Therapist,
Richmond State Psychiatric Hospital

Norman Falcone, Activity Therapist Director,
Richmond State Psychiatric Hospital

The late Dr. R.D. Laing, Visiting Psychiatrist,
Bellevue Psychiatric Hospital

Jane Cassidy, Activity Therapy Director,
Bellevue Psychiatric Hospital

Suzanne Patterson, OTR,
Activity Therapy Director, Bellevue Psychiatric

Elaine Bill, Receptionist, Bellevue Psychiatric Hospital

Rudolph Thomas, M.S., Activity Therapist,
Bellevue Psychiatric Hospital

Frank Conanan, M.S., Activity Therapist,
Bellevue Psychiatric Hospital

Gertrude Schattner, Drama Therapist,
Bellevue Psychiatric Hospital

Charles Nance, Music Therapist,
Bellevue Psychiatric Hospital

Judith Ackerman, Dance Therapist,
Bellevue Psychiatric Hospital

Remi Gay, Dance Therapist,
Bellevue Psychiatric Hospital

Nina Robinson, Dance Therapist,
Bellevue Psychiatric Hospital

Thanks also to J. M. Sirko & Associates, Inc.
for her precise and final editing of the book.